MOUNTAIN BIKING

Raintree www.raintreepublishers.co.uk

To order:
Phone 44 (0) 1865 888112
Send a fax to 44 (0) 1865 314091
Visit the Raintree bookshop at
www.raintreepublishers.co.uk
to browse our catalogue and order online.

Produced by
David West Children's Books
7 Princeton Court
55 Felsham Road
London SW15 1AZ

Picture Research: Carlotta Cooper
Designer: Gary Jeffrey
Editor: James Pickering

First published in Great Britain by
Raintree, Halley Court, Jordan Hill,
Oxford OX2 8EJ, part of Harcourt Education.
Raintree is a registered trademark of Harcourt
Education Ltd.

© David West Children's Books 2003
The moral right of the proprietor has been asserted.

Printed and bound in Italy

ISBN 1 844 43090 1 (hardback)
07 06 05 04 03
10 9 8 7 6 5 4 3 2 1

ISBN 1 844 43095 2 (paperback)
08 07 06 05 04
10 9 8 7 6 5 4 3 2 1

British Library Cataloguing in Publication Data
Osborne, Ian
Mountain Biking. – (Extreme sports)
796.6'3
A full catalogue record for this book is available
from the British Library.

Acknowledgements
The publishers would like to thank the following
for permission to reproduce photographs:

Abbreviations: t-top, m-middle, b-bottom, r-right,
l-left, c-centre.

Front cover - Corbis Images. Pages 3, 5, 7b, 8 both,
9tl, bl & br, 10-11 both, 11 all, 12t, 13 all, 14tl &
bl, 15t & m, 16b, 17l, 18t, 19 both, 20t, 21tl & r,
22t & bl, 23tr, 24t, 25br, 26-27, 27tl & br, 28
both, 28-29, 29 all - Ian Osborne. 4-5 - Helen
Mortimer. 6 both, 6-7, 7t - Wendy Cragg. 7m, 14m
& br, 16t, 22br, 27tr & bl, 30bl - Corbis Images.
9tr - Digital Stock. 12b, 15b, 17t & b, 23tl & b -
Buzz Pictures. 24-25t, 25m, 26m - Jonathan
Gawler.

Every effort has been made to contact copyright
holders of any material reproduced in this book.
Any omissions will be rectified in subsequent
printings if notice is given to the publishers.

*An explanation of difficult words can be
found in the glossary on page 31.*

extreme sports

MOUNTAIN BIKING

Ian Osborne

Raintree

CONTENTS

Introduction

Mountain bikes are the most common bikes bought by young people today. Over the last 30 years, mountain biking has grown into an international and Olympic sport. Some lucky riders even earn their livings from mountain biking. Whether you're a top racer or just playing in the dirt, the adrenaline buzz is the same. Riders can specialize in different areas of the sport. You might want to ride off-road to get fit, see beautiful countryside, get a thrill from downhill and dirt jumping or just have fun with your friends - mountain biking has it all.

SKY HIGH
A backflip is a backwards spin in mid-air.

WARNING!
MOUNTAIN BIKING CAN BE AN **EXTREMELY DANGEROUS** SPORT. DO NOT ATTEMPT ANY MOVES **BEYOND YOUR ABILITIES** AND ALWAYS WEAR THE APPROPRIATE SAFETY EQUIPMENT.

ROUGH RIDE
Helen Mortimer wears leg protection during a race.

No single person invented mountain biking. But in the early 1970s, a group of riders took their bikes off-road in Marin County, California and developed a hobby that became a worldwide craze.

How it all started

This group of riders held untimed and unplanned races at Mount Tamalpais. Over time, more people took an interest in this new style of cycling and more races were held. With each race, the riders would customize their bikes to make them more suitable for the tough terrain. The most popular bike was a heavyweight balloon-tyred model, chosen for its strength and handling. These bikes were fondly known as 'clunkers'.

☻ ON TOP OF THE WORLD
A mountain bike can take you to astonishing places.

☻ DOWNHILL SLIDE
To take a downhill corner, you need to slide into the curve.

Mass production

In the early 1980s, bikes began to be produced on a large scale. Mike Sinyard of 'Specialized Bikes' bought an early custom-made frame, and took the idea to Japan. The first bike he made was called the Stump Jumper. This was an expensive bike, but it sold thousands in its first two years. By the mid 1980s, mountain bike sales overtook road bike sales, and the sport was here to stay.

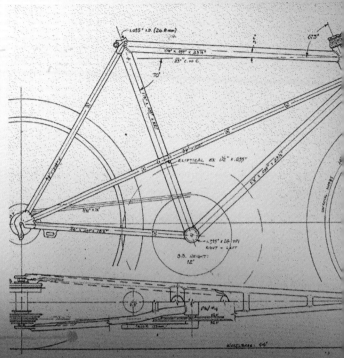

SKETCHED OUT
This Custom Cruiser mountain bike was designed by Joe Breeze in 1977.

GREAT OUTDOORS
For many, being close to nature is mountain biking's greatest appeal.

HARD WORK
Riders pushed their bikes to the top of a mountain and raced them down dirt tracks. With bikes weighing in excess of 30kg, this was hard work, especially with no gears. Over time, riders added gears and other modifications. The first mountain bike frames were developed in the mid-1970s.

GUIDE #1

GARY FISHER
Gary Fisher was one of the early pioneers of mountain biking. He was one of the best riders, and also went on to develop his own frames and a bike company. This company still exists today and Gary is one of the most colourful characters in the industry. Gary can still be seen racing bikes, and one of his sponsored riders, Paola Pezzo, has won two Olympic gold medals.

RIDER AND DESIGNER
Gary sponsors (pays) people to ride his bikes.

Evolution - types of riding

Over time, mountain biking has split into many different areas. Today, you can ride cross-country, downhill and on the street. You can take part in bicycle supercross, dirt jumping, trials and races.

Cross-country and downhill

In a cross-country race, you compete on a set course, usually for several hours, taking in hill climbs, downhill sections and single tracks. This form of racing is now an Olympic discipline. Downhill racing developed from cross-country. It's a thrilling, high-speed form of biking. Riders race against the clock over a short, rocky course. Races usually last no longer than six minutes.

☺ BUMPY RIDE
Bicycle supercross races usually last less than a minute.

Bicycle supercross

In bicycle supercross, or duel racing, two or more riders race against each other over a short jump-littered course, similar to a BMX track. This is a tough and highly competitive form of mountain biking.

☺ SINGLE TRACK
Cross-country tracks are narrow, with plenty of bumps.

ROCK DROP

A trials rider drops from the top of a high rock.

Dirt jumping and trials

Riders often like to take their bikes off-road and jump them. This is called dirt jumping, and it takes place at dirt jump trails, where riders have dug several sets of double jumps to form packs. The riders then jump over each double, letting go of their bikes, flipping as they go through the packs. In a mountain bike trial, riders test their balancing skills, as they hop and jump their bikes over a specially designed course. They must try not to put a foot down while riding through the obstacles on the course. The street is a popular training ground for mountain bike trials.

GUIDE #2

OTHER DISCIPLINES

Adventure and 24-hour racing

Riders' skill and stamina are tested by adventure and 24-hour races. Adventure races take in map and compass work as the riders move from one checkpoint to the next. 24-hour races take place over a day and riders race for a 24-hour period in teams. Really tough riders even race solo for 24 hours!

Street riding and freeriding

As their name suggests, street riders ride their bikes in towns and cities, using walls, steps and barriers to create a whole new playground. Freeriding is the newest and fastest-growing type of mountain biking. Riders take their bikes to remote locations and 'free' ride the natural terrain.

AIRBORNE

Dirt jumpers often do spins on trails.

Equipment – bikes

Each area of mountain biking has its own styles of bike, equipment and fashions linked to it. Improved technology means that bikes are now faster than ever, and also more reliable and easier to ride.

Light, yet strong, race frame

Cross-country bikes

Lightweight bikes are best for cross-country, adventure and 24-hour racing. These are designed to be fast and easy to pedal for mile after mile. They have up to 27 gears for going up and down the steepest hills. The tyres on these bikes are very narrow for extra speed.

Downhill bikes

For fast riding over rocky terrain, downhill bikes need to be super-strong. They have big tyres, nine gears, disc brakes and strong suspension to make the ride smoother (see page 31). Similar style bikes are used by the more extreme freeriders.

HARDTAIL
A hardtail bike has no suspension on the rear wheel.

Low seat for ease of movement

Dual crown front suspension fork

Strong aluminium suspension frame

DOWNHILL SET-UP
Downhill bikes are some of the heaviest mountain bikes.

Lightweight suspension fork

Bicycle supercross bikes

In bicycle supercross contests, riders use a bike that's a mixture between a cross-country and a downhill bike. These tough, short suspension, travel bikes are strong enough to take plenty of punishment. But they're also light, so riders can pedal very quickly.

SUPERCROSS
Supercross bikes are used for sprint racing.

Dirt jump bikes

To survive the treatment its rider dishes out, a dirt jump bike needs to be as strong as possible. Strong hardtail frames with short travel suspension forks and few frills make up this simple yet super-tough little bike. Often they have only nine gears. Truly hardcore jumpers use bikes with just one speed, so there are no gear mechanisms to get broken.

Super-strong frame

TOUGH CUSTOMER
The frame of a dirt jump bike is made of steel.

Tough single crown forks

Trials bikes

These bikes are lightweight yet strong. The gearing system enables riders to pedal instantly from a balance point or up very steep rocks. Riders use hydraulic or disc brakes for instant stopping power.

TRIALS BIKE
The gearing system is easy to use.

Mountain bike hotspots

You can go mountain biking all over the world. Whether it's jumping off the kerb in the street, or exploring a foreign country, riders are always searching for new, faster and even more extreme situations.

Places to ride

Mountain bike hotspots have developed throughout the world and certain places should be on every mountain biker's wish list to ride. Moab in Utah, USA is one such place. Its odd-looking slick rock and many routes draw thousands of visitors. Another great US attraction is New England, especially Vermont and New Hampshire. Further west, Arizona offers some of the most spectacular mountain biking scenery in the world.

California is the birth place of mountain biking. This western state offers all sorts of riding experiences, from great scenic day rides through to downhill, dirt jump spots and bicycle supercross courses.

FREEDOM
Freeriding means riding new and untouched terrain.

Europe

The Alps in Europe offer some of the best downhill, cross-country and day rides. The nearby Pyrenees also attract many riders, who come for the beautiful landscape and great trails, which you can reach by lift or train.

CLOSE TO NATURE
Taking your bike off the streets is a great way of discovering the natural world.

Racing

World Cup races in downhill, cross-country and bicycle supercross take place all over the world including North America, Europe, Australia and parts of Asia. This whole colourful travelling circus of riders, trucks, mechanics and team managers has also visited Japan and Sweden – countries not usually associated with the sport. Many of the people who come to watch races, or see them on television, are tempted to have a go themselves. The result is that mountain biking, especially off-road, is getting more and more popular all the time.

POINTS EAST

This downhill race is taking place in Slovenia, eastern Europe.

FAR FROM HOME

Bikes can be easily packed away for long distance travel. This Canadian rider is exploring in France.

GUIDE #3

SKI RESORTS

These days, riders can take their bikes to ski and snowboard resorts in the summer. The natural terrain makes these ideal destinations. Mountain bikers can transport their bikes on chairlifts, in cars and even in helicopters to the most remote spots. Ski resorts are especially popular with downhillers, freeriders and day trippers. Riding a bike in these far-flung places would have been unthinkable just a few years ago.

Clothing and equipment

Off-road mountain biking is a potentially dangerous sport, and bikers usually wear safety equipment to help prevent any serious injuries. Only a fool thinks it's cool not to wear a helmet and gloves at the very least.

Cross-country kit

An open face helmet and gloves are the only protection worn by cross-country riders. They wear skin-tight shorts and jerseys made from aerodynamic Lycra material, which doesn't get caught up in the bike and allows moisture to escape as they sweat. Their shorts have a padded insert called a chamois to protect them from discomfort during all those miles spent sweating on the saddle.

Internal hip guards

Elbow guards

SAFE AND SOUND
Gloves are essential to protect your hands from blisters and crash injuries.

HEAD PROTECTION
An open face helmet is the bare minimum of protection you should wear when riding.

Lycra shorts with padded insert

Lycra shirt with zip front and rear pockets

Downhill, freeride and BSX kit

Crashes are very common in downhill, freeride and bicycle supercross (BSX) races because of the high speeds riders reach over the toughest terrain. To protect their heads, they wear full face helmets similar to a motocross rider, and goggles to stop anything flying into their eyes. They wear body armour to protect their backs and chests. Along with this, they wear elbow guards, knee and shin pads.

A full face helmet is a must for the dangers of downhill racing.

Dirt, street and trials kit

Knee and shin pads

Riders in dirt, street and trials contests don't wear too much in the way of safety equipment, but you will nearly always see them with a helmet and gloves. Knee and shin pads are often used, because if a pedal slams into your leg it can cause a nasty accident. These riders usually wear skateboard-influenced shoes that offer plenty of padding and support around the ankle, as well as good heel protection to take the sting out of those heavy landings.

BODY PROTECTION
Body armour protects your ribs and spine.

GUIDE #4

FREAKY FASHIONS

During the last 30 years or so, mountain biking has seen some good and some truly hideous fashion trends. Bikers moved on from jeans, hike boots and facial hair to skin-tight Lycra suits, silly tasselled hats, patterned print neon and huge sunglasses.

The two-piece suit was never standard riding gear.

Basic techniques

Whatever type of riding you do, your basic technique will help you stay on the bike and feel more confident. If you're going downhill, slugging it out uphill or trying to get round a corner, you must learn to use your brakes.

Braking

Skilled mountain bikers use their brakes to keep their bikes under control. The front brake has the greatest stopping power, but it should never be grabbed too sharply or the front wheel will lock up and send you over the bars. Similarly, if you grab the rear brake too sharply it will lock the back wheel and cause the bike to skid. This will leave the rear wheel out of control and wear out the tyres.

EASY DOES IT

You should use both your brakes together to slow down in a gentle and controlled way.

Uphill technique

To ride uphill you'll need strong legs and plenty of puff. As you sit on the saddle, you need to keep your weight central and have a smooth-spinning pedal action. Try to find the balance point between the front wheel popping up (which means your weight is too far back) and your rear wheel spinning on the ground (which means your weight is too far forwards).

GET A GRIP

When riding uphill, you must keep your weight balanced so the rear wheel doesn't lose traction, and the bike doesn't flip over.

Downhill technique

It's important to keep your weight back when riding down steep terrain. Push your bottom back over the rear tyre (not on it though!) to keep the bike balanced. Find your centre of gravity and keep your arms bent so that you can control the bike while in this position. If you're too far forwards, you could go over the bars. Remember to keep the pedals level so they don't catch rocks or roots.

Cornering

You must remember to control your speed before you arrive at a corner. If you wait until the last minute to brake, the bike might skid out of control. Brake early and lift the pedals so the inside pedal is at the top of the pedal stroke. Put your weight on the outside pedal at the bottom of the stroke and lean into the corner. Your weight on the tyres gives them grip.

CORNERING
Lift the inside pedal and push on the outside one when taking a corner.

KEEP WELL BACK
To avoid a front flip, keep your weight as far back as possible.

GUIDE #5

ARM AND LEG SUSPENSION

Use your knees and elbows as suspension when you're out of the saddle. To do this, keep your pedals level while relaxing and bending your knees and elbows. This helps to feed the bike comfortably through the terrain, while you remain in a position in which it's easy to control the bike.

With knees and arms bent, your body will absorb any bumps.

Maintenance and set-up

Setting up and looking after your bike correctly will mean years of happy riding. It will also save you a lot of money on new parts and servicing. Firstly you should set your bike up for the style of riding you're doing.

Basic set-up

If you want to race cross-country or go for a long ride, the saddle should be at the correct height. When you're sitting on the bike with the pedal at the bottom of the stroke, your leg should be almost straight but with a slight bend in the knee. Downhillers, jumpers, supercross racers and street riders have their seats lower.

To obtain the correct seat height, lean against a wall and drop one pedal. Your leg should have a slight bend in it.

5

4

2

3

1

Basic maintenance

The bike has moving parts that require lubrication. Mud and water are the bike's worst enemies. You should clean your bike with soapy water after every ride, especially if it's wet or muddy.

For pedals, headsets, suspension and bottom brackets, leave any repairs to your local bike shop.

GUIDE #6

PEDALS

Flat pedals are similar to the pedals on a regular bike. These are favoured by beginners, along with dirt jumpers, trial and street riders, freeriders and some downhillers who need to take their feet off quickly. Clipless pedals use a cleat on the bottom of your shoes and a clipless mechanism on the pedal. When the two are engaged you are part of the bike. This enables you to pull on the upstroke of the pedal turn, which gives more power. These are favoured by day riders, cross country riders and some downhillers. You can unclip easily by twisting your shoes sideways.

Flat pedals with pins to grip your shoes

Clipless pedals with quick release mechanism for shoes

GUIDE #7

PARTS OF THE BIKE

1 Three gear chainset

2 Seven gear hub

3 Rear fork's swing-arm joint

4 Rear shock absorber

5 Rigid aluminium frame

6 Front brake disc

7 Disc brake

8 Front fork's shock absorber

Intermediate techniques

Grabbing some air is what every mountain biker craves. You can do this by launching yourself from a jump or by dropping off a sheer ledge in a controlled fall. The size of your jump depends on your speed.

Grabbing air

It's what you do in the air that makes the difference between a smooth landing and ending up on the ground. Start out small and learn your style. When you hit a jump, pull up on the bars to stop the front end from nose diving. Try to keep your weight central, hold on and relax. Look where you're going to touch down and try to land both wheels at the same time.

LOOKING GOOD

It's not enough just to grab air – try to look stylish at the same time.

GUIDE #8
HOW TO WHEELIE

Ride along slowly and pull up on the bars while leaning back.

Once the front wheel is up, find your balance point.

Speed jumping

Pull up on the bars to lift the front wheel, so that it clears the top of the jump. As it does, push back down to place the wheel on the down side of the jump. Push your weight back to keep the rear wheel on the ground. As it passes over the top of the jump, put your weight forwards and start to pedal again.

Drop offs

Ride with the pedals level and pull up on the bars as you leave the edge, to stop the front end from diving. Try to land on both wheels for a smooth landing. Use your arms and legs to absorb the impact.

ROCK STEADY

A rider performs a drop off with the front end up and the weight central.

LOW LEVEL

Keeping the bike on or close to the ground is the fastest way of taking a jump.

If the wheel is coming up too high, lightly tap the rear brake to bring it down.

If the wheel is falling, push on the pedals and pull on the bars to bring it back up.

You've got a bike and all the shiny new kit. It's time to ride but where do you go? You don't have to live in one of the mountain bike hotspots or travel the world to get a kick out of riding.

PLAN AHEAD
The journey downhill can be more challenging than the uphill ride.

Rivers and canal paths

These routes are great for beginners. River and canal paths can offer great views and there are never any major hills. Plus there are plenty of entry and exit points so you can ride for as long or as briefly as you like.

RIVER RIDING
River banks often flood. Check tide times before setting out.

Designated trails

Designated mountain bike courses and trail routes are listed in most mountain bike magazines. Your local bike shop should also be able to point you in the right direction. Some routes are free to use, while others will ask for a small fee to help towards their upkeep. There are routes to ride all over the place, depending on how far you're willing to travel.

ROUGH RIDE
Designated trails can offer some of the most challenging riding.

Extreme
Caution
Severe
Downhill

BMX tracks are the perfect places to try out your skills.

BMX tracks and waste ground

For those seeking more of a thrill, why not look for the local BMX track? These have jumps, tabletops, beams and all sorts of technical obstacles to practise on. Waste ground or open land on the outskirts of town can provide natural obstacles where you can sharpen your skills. Remember to stay safe.

BUMPY RIDE

The obstacles on waste ground can be as dangerous as in parks, so always wear safety equipment.

GUIDE #9

FITNESS

You don't have to be a wiry cross-country racer or a burly downhiller to ride mountain bikes. Fitness comes with time spent in the saddle and there's no better way to get fit than by riding a bike. Start out with short, easy rides and build up to bigger things. Make sure you give your body time to rest before the next ride.

Advanced techniques

Now it's time to start putting some style into your riding. The techniques and skills you need are similar, regardless of what sort of mountain biking you do. Here are some of the coolest tricks young people can do on a mountain bike.

Jumping - removing hands and feet

Once you have the basic jump skills, you could think about removing your hands, feet or even both in mid-air. These are among the first styles jumpers learn in the advanced stage. Build up to this by removing your limbs just a little, before you start extending arms and legs while you jump.

CANCAN

A rider performs a double foot cancan in the middle of a jump.

GUIDE #10

HOW TO BUNNY-HOP

Ride along slowly with pedals level and pull up on the bars.

The back wheel will leave the ground and you'll be in the air with both wheels off the ground.

The front wheel will lift off the ground. As it does, push forwards on the bars and scoop up the back wheel using your feet on the pedals.

Street riding - wall rides

Street riders jump off huge blocks, ride up walls and hop over big gaps. To ride a wall, ride at an angle and pull up on the handle bars while bunny-hopping up on to the wall. Let your wheels ride the wall, before pulling on the bars again to exit the wall. Land on both wheels and ride away.

💀 WALL RIDE
A simple brick wall in the street can make a challenging obstacle.

Jumping - 360s

To make the bike spin a full 360 degrees, you need to turn into the jump and twist your head and upper body in the direction you wish to spin. The bike will rotate naturally with your body, and stop when you do.

💀 HIGH SPIN
This rider is half way through spinning 360 degrees.

Trials - hopping off blocks

Pull up on the bars so the bike is on the rear wheel. Hop forwards while pulling on the bars as the bike leaves the top of the block. Let the rear wheel touch down first. Then allow the front wheel to touch down.

💀 TRIALS
A trials rider hops off an indoor block.

Try to land on both wheels at the same time to complete the bunny-hop.

Safety and equipment

Mountains are dangerous places. The weather can change at any time and make it very difficult to navigate. It's important to pack the right equipment to help you get back to base safely.

Map and compass

The first thing you need is a map. Mark your route on the map before you leave, and study where you're going. A compass will point you in the right direction. These are inexpensive items, but they could save your life.

PREPARATION
A map tells you the height of the terrain you want to ride on.

TECHNOLOGY
A GPS fitted to a bike makes navigation easy.

GPS (Global Positioning System)

A GPS is an expensive piece of equipment that tracks you, via a satellite in space. If you get lost and have a map, the GPS will tell you where you are. It will also navigate your route for you, and help you to find your way back. These are great if you're heading into unknown terrain for a big ride in the mountains, or freeriding in the outback.

SPACE AGE
The GPS is constantly keeping track of where you and your bike are.

Clothing

It's very important to take the right clothing for your ride. It may be shorts and t-shirt weather at the bottom of the mountain, but it gets colder the higher you climb. So make sure you have some warmer clothing with you in case it gets too cold. A waterproof jacket will protect you against sudden mountain storms.

Hydration pack   Waterproof

Fleece

Map

Pump

Tools

Spare tube

Tools

You also need a basic tool kit in case your bike goes wrong. Compact multi tools work for most repairs. It's also important to take a spare inner tube and a pump in case you get a puncture.

ALL YOU NEED

This is the essential kit for a day out riding in the mountains.

KEEPING WARM

Fleeces let skin breathe, they are warm and very light.

GUIDE #11

WATER

Riding a bike makes you sweat. It's important to replace the water you're losing. This is called hydration. The only way to do this is to drink lots of water. There are many different kinds of hydration system, from the simple water bottle to the hydration backpack. This has an internal bladder with a drinking tube on the shoulder strap for you to swig from.

Hydration pack with internal water bladder and drinking tube

Stars of the sport

Mountain bike racing has created some huge stars. They travel the world, all expenses paid, and race bikes in glamorous locations. You might think this is a dream job, but you need plenty of determination to reach the top.

Anne Caroline Chausson (France)

This former BMX race world champion is the greatest female rider in mountain biking. She has won more World Championship series titles than any other woman, in both downhill and bicycle supercross. When she isn't racing, Anne enjoys grabbing some air on the dirt jumps.

CHAUSSON
Anne has also won the most World Cup titles.

Brian Lopes (USA)

This young American is usually at the front of the pack in any race. Brian Lopes is the hottest star of bicycle supercross racing, and has won more races than anyone else in this discipline. Brian has also won both the World Championships and the overall World Cup series in bicycle supercross.

LOPES
Brian started racing bikes at the age of four.

Greg Minnaar (South Africa)

Greg Minnaar won the World Cup series in 2001 – the youngest rider ever to achieve this. Greg is a stylish racer and jumper who is usually in the top ten of any World Cup race, though injuries have recently slowed down his progress. Greg rides for the Global Racing Mountain Bike team.

MINNAAR
Greg was only 19 when he won the World Cup series.

Nicolas Vouilloz (France)

Nine times world champion, Nicolas Vouilloz has unbelievable speed and a gentle style. As well as racing himself, Nicolas has started his own team and helps young racers find their potential.

🏆 **VOUILLOZ**
Nicolas has also won five World Cup titles.

Steve Peat (UK)

This laid back native of Sheffield, South Yorkshire, is one of the most consistent riders on the circuit. Steve has won many World Cup races and came second in the World Championships. He also came second in the World Cup series. It's just a matter of time before he wins a championship.

🏆 **PEAT**
Steve Peat is the UK's best downhiller.

Paola Pezzo (Italy)

Paola Pezzo is the biggest name in women's cross-country racing. She has won both the World Cup series and the World Championships during her career. Paola has also won two gold medals in the Olympic Games – a feat no other rider has ever achieved.

🏆 **PEZZO**
During the 1997 season, Paola won every race she entered.

Today, mountain biking is one of the most popular sports in the world. You don't have to be a champion BSX rider to make the most of your bike – you can have just as much fun in town, or riding at weekends to keep yourself in shape. There are plenty of publications and websites that can point you in the right direction.

PLACES TO RIDE

Britain has some spectacular trails. The North Downs Way and the Surrey Hills are within easy reach of London. Further north, the North York Moors National Park and the West Highland Way in Scotland are popular with holidaymakers.

Australia boasts many routes near its major cities, such as the Blue Mountains in New South Wales and the Brisbane Forest Park in Queensland.

Moab, Utah, USA is a major mountain biking hotspot. There are many different routes for all abilities and tastes. For further information, go to www.moab-utah.com.

Arizona has hundreds of legal trails, catering for all types of riders. Get hold of Cosmic Ray's guide – *Fat Tyre Trails and Tails*. This humorous insight also contains extensive maps of the area.

Les Gets, Morzine offers downhill, freeriding and day riding in the heart of the French Alps. Access to courses is free, although if you want to use the ski lifts you will need to buy a pass. Log on to www.alpactive.com.

MAGAZINES & PERIODICALS

Mountain Biking UK

Future Publishing, 30 Monmouth Street, Bath,
 BA1 2BW, UK
 Tel: 00 44 1225 442 244

The UK's best-selling mountain bike magazine, covering all areas of the sport with racing, interviews, routes to ride, product and bike testing.

Dirt

4130 Publishing PO Box 1300, Dorchester,
 Dorset, DT1 1FN, UK
 Tel: 00 44 1305 251 263

Dirt covers downhill, dirt jumping and BSX racing with top quality pictures, bike and product tests and coverage of mountain bike racing.

Mountain Bike

West: 2059 Empire Ave, Suite 2, Burbank,
 CA, 91504, USA
 Tel: 00 1 818 953 8730
East: 135 North Sixth St, Emmaus, PA, 18098, USA
 Tel 00 1 610 967 5171

Mountain Bike is one of the best American mountain bike magazines. This publication covers all areas of the sport, accompanied by beautiful pictures.

USEFUL WEBSITES

www.alpactive.com

www.bcf.uk.com

www.bikemagic.com

www.bsxworld.com

www.descent-world.co.uk

www.dhrace.com

www.ecochallenge.com

www.freeridetours.com

www.imba.com

www.mbuk.com

www.mountainbike.com

www.mtbbritain.co.uk

www.singletrackworld.com

www.trailsource.com

All the Internet addresses (URLs) given in this book were valid at the time of going to press. However, due to the dynamic nature of the Internet, some addresses may have changed, or sites may have ceased to exist since publication. While the author and publishers regret any inconvenience this may cause readers, no responsibility for any such changes can be accepted by either the author or the publishers.

Glossary

aerodynamic

describes the movement of air around an object, and how much wind resistance it has. A highly aerodynamic bike will cut through the air quickly and efficiently.

aluminium

lightweight metal, used for making mountain bike frames and components

BSX

bicycle supercross – a race with many contenders over a short course, with jumps

customize

modify and improve

disc brake

braking system that uses wheel-mounted discs, as on a modern car, rather than pads, which grip the rim of the tyre

fork

part of the bike that holds the front wheels, and is used for steering

freeriding

riding new and untouched terrain

gears

mechanism that moves the chain over cogs of different sizes, which makes pedalling a bike harder or easier. Generally, lower gears are used for travelling uphill, and higher ones for travelling downhill.

grabbing air

any trick on a bike when both wheels leave the ground

hydraulic

system that works using water or oil pressure

lubrication

covering of oil or grease to make a surface smooth

Lycra

smooth, skintight fabric used to make sports clothing

open face helmet

helmet without a chin guard

shock absorber

suspension device used to cushion hard impacts

suspension

system of springs and dampers that keep the bike steady over rough ground for a smooth and steady ride

terrain

environment or type of ground where you ride

titanium

expensive, lightweight metal, used for making bike frames and parts

Index

MOUNTAIN BIKING